Took House

Lauren Camp

Took House

Lauren Camp

Tupelo Press

Took House
Copyright © 2020 Lauren Camp. All rights reserved.

Library of Congress Catalog-in-Publication data available upon request.
ISBN-13: 978-1-946482-32-7

Cover image: Suzanne Sbarge, "Nest," 2005, mixed media on panel.
Used by permission of the artist.
Cover and text design by Kenji Liu.

First paperback edition August 2020

Tupelo Press
P.O. Box 1767
North Adams, Massachusetts 01247
(413) 664-9611 / Fax: (413) 664-9711
editor@tupelopress.org / www.tupelopress.org

Tupelo Press is an award-winning independent literary press that publishes fine fiction, non-fiction, and poetry in books that are a joy to hold as well as read. Tupelo Press is a registered 501(c)(3) nonprofit organization, and we rely on public support to carry out our mission of publishing extraordinary work that may be outside the realm of the large commercial publishers. Financial donations are welcome and are tax deductible.

CONTENTS

DAYS AT ZERO

"My right or wrong isn't
to have a pure or fine edge."

—Eva Hesse

Appetite

And now in the useless unceasing, there is a heart

in one part of town, where there is a table
that is most like a cliff, a place to render

fewer potentials. There is a glass

near a bottle that will offer what she asks.
In that room, or the next, is an intimate slowing

where the woman put down her shield
and took out her heart. She put it on the table

and looked at the table under the eye

of everything that could go wrong,
everything that did,

each direct chance and the taking of it.
Now she tries to explain

the way the past wouldn't finish,

that the heart was a stipulation, the shade

of her hunger, his palm on her marrow. It is the largest
muscle and she let it

take over, she let it.

The Exact Color of Welcome

Find the Color of Survival

I want to talk about what I believe
is beautiful, and this is complicated by all the oil

of that year. The muscle of my mind
was worn out. I was painting everything at once,

painting until the impulse died,
and began again. I tended to let days scatter

to bruises on canvas—absolute color
the temperature I tolerated,

and my hands the only source
of compassion. My eyes stayed on the symbols

of other artists' corners and saw as they spread
to a world that existed

through another parking lot, a skein
of grasses. Four shades of green could halve

and bend the eye. Even in excess
I always see the most trivial details. Even then,

I was always sure a return to heaven's
brightness. These are the matters

for which there are no limits. How far imagination
commands and I splendored

over it. I starved to praise, contented
in the ways of light and bed and silhouette

because I had sacrificed
to muddy palms an art inscribed with truth

and the dominion of hues, the breathless
blue. I believe you'll see in every image

pleasure and twenty different senses.
Every past in the right

and wrong place, so many times no one can tell
if they saw us. A woman tying a black apron

brought the cutlery to our table;
at home I lifted a broad brush to each sorrow.

One day soon every form will be transparent—
but first, with you I'm looking

at even what I cannot stand to see.

Leather World, This Bird, This Sky

I came here from temporary
and perpetual rages—the whole sky
of wind. Secret birds
take the ruin of garden.
Hail carefully cuts out
the unseen side, the open veins.
Dirt offers its fragrance
through flooding.
When the nest falls,
I open the twigs and find only
crickets with their gasps
and clicking. For 19 years I have been
driving toward reason—or into
the sinews of city: the pile-up
on the interstate, the drums
of hydrochloric acid
near intersections, the suspicion.
Where does it end?
I've always understood
what can't be said, but the man
who complained of kindness
had to apologize. There's almost
no dialogue between life's
various promises. Such endeavor,
all of these seasons.
Wind pulls on one wing
then a next—and a raptor flies
crooked through its mandolin language.
Suddenly everything verified:
cloud without end.

The Night Clouds Wrestled the Sky

At that moment, I was blind to the sorrow
      and stop that was coming.
            For that gentle hour, I settled
into the only split in the road

where I still saw the purple reflection of day
      slipping from cedar and aspen.
            Air temperature as skin would shift
to bare and brisk. But in the sky, unguarded

orange shadows advanced, and clouds extended
      to unkempt corners, the desert's chambers of gray.
            Trees unfurled their fluted, five-petaled,
veined fingers. Precision worth noting.

What else should we look at but fugitive color,
      the shape that's not empty?
            So little of what happens belongs to us,
only the frequent sense of being encircled.

After light was stripped from the scarlet wall,
      a string of birds armed long branches,
            rhapsodizing. I had entered the chatter-
curved worship of their bursting, the song grafted

to the moon's musky discipline.
      Once their noise was placed, it remained
            in my mind—for years. Not a coincidence
that I heard and saw a final stray sweep of sun

as pigment and chord, and would summon it again
      next time I was swallowed, beat down.
            That night the sky came up to my lips.
It tasted of wind, and gave me something to miss.

Draw a Box

INSPIRED BY SOL LEWITT'S WALL DRAWINGS

On the white wall of your heart, a box.
  Without a ruler, I draw.

Within the box a word. Anything you choose.
  I write moan, lace, seed pod, stumble.

Draw a circle that reaches the edges but does not exit
the box, then a vertiginous series of lines rising over a valley.
  To the east, sun tips up as though in a memory.

Watch someone you know approach the box
from the northeast edge by the wooden bridge.
Quickly draw a door on your box.
  Wearing black silk gloves,
  a small, beautiful woman reaches for the door.

Listen to the cerulean sound of her swallows.
  The tones swoop forward, and settle on the ceiling.

When she exits, watch her walk up the steep hill
to a brick house you hadn't seen before.
  Under her arm, she holds an old delphinium
  she found in the box.

Turn off the lights in your box.

Feel the missing sides of the box.

Repetitions

Each I were we—there or here without
one person. With another and ferocious
to them. Each I flowered outward

       and he and I knew what was being done with
       one person—and ferocious

most to that other. Dark thoughts and doorways
and we knew what was being done
this side of flesh, both now straying to

       most of another. Dark thoughts and doorways
       crossed together. We bent and fell

this side of flesh, both now straying to
a last precipice, which we'd only
cross together. We'd promised. We bent and fell

       and were again more than one and one
       at a last precipice, which we would never

have thought to do to each other and we swore
never again more than one and one
to the other. Each I might flower outward

       but wouldn't reach to another and we swore
       each I would be this we—there or here.

Remember It Was

I will speak of this wind: name it *continent*, name it

dredging. I will speak
of the seams of desire, the practice

and even the ceiling. I was 27 when I belonged

by my heart. I was
later older with the invasion. Because of the birds and the rapture

and colors. I'll never—

still sometimes another   or others   and repeated.

Splendid

Yes, it was splendid, praying holy
with liquor to the twelve-bar pattern
of his tragic. Our hands and fingers,
the interior weather, such latent languor.
The waiter was never far from the mouth
of our error and ready to please us,
to place fuller glasses beside us,
filled with disorder. Over and over
we sat at a table without days,
our lips scarlet with logic
and random syntax. We sat through
summer's collar, sat through sweet mustard
and drought, my soft opinions,
his signatures, then winter's slaughtering
wind spread on the desert.
We perfected hours: our small infinities
and unremarkable habits. The flesh,
our last words. Of course,
at some point, we at the table
were reminded only of breathing:
that echo and echo.

Smote

Give me your flowered ear. Did you see how I carried my breath in a handbag and peeled off the parts of myself he requested? May I never again need to be so fluent in silk at daylight. Festering boil. Disease of the crops.

Take handfuls of ashes...

Give me the bitter in chances. Noon turned to smudges. We sat by the wall, taking desire as treasure to the back of our throats. We had light in Goshen, and stream and cloud—

> *May there be blood,*
> *   the worst hailstorm—*

Much later, I count these plagues down, how the moon hardly wobbled through vowel on vowel, through windowpane, the mountains forgotten, my home full of torment. I confess: the small form of my body found sweetness. The sky at my door, the legs of the chair. We weren't yet finished. I was devoured
for months. I knew why I had gone—

> *and if thou refuse to let them go, behold, I will smite*
> *   all the borders*

But I made it home through the dust where the sun tumbled in and lifted out as it sometimes does.

Hush, Then

This is not about the narrow streets. Not about the creeping cold. I drove along the road and up and over with my headlights, with hurtles and verticals, my eyes on the radio backbeats, the homeless, the waltz of the ravens. It was nearly enough—to reach a dark room and a number of days in one afternoon. Every week this dangling, a pouring of bottles. The door found its exit but stayed half inside when I ambled over stones to watch the pitch of his mouth, my name when he said it, a point of view I accepted. The cadence when he asked for my gasps. My answer needed statistics, but I couldn't manage the math, so offered the exact color of a smile. He took that as welcome. At the table, the knives were all clean. At the table, any minute was borrowed. And I leaned back and saw blue in the shiny corners of eyes where no one asked which and no one said who.

Tar Painting

INSPIRED BY JUDY TUWALETSTIWA, *TEXT: BLOOD/EARTH*, 2001, TAR, STRAW AND OTHER MEDIA

Alice showed us her house and the slight delicate light
that collapsed on each surface, each sofa.

My new friend showed us her lonely rooms.
My vision narrowed to rows of pre-Colombian pots

and a black painting in a long niche by the bedroom.
Art was everywhere tethered to walls.

Alice served salmon with a crisp crust.
I drank the gin-clear water and agonized about forks.

As we ate, we discussed how many black moments it takes
to fill a vessel of betrayal. Without prying, I knew

her husband had been removed, the kitchen renovated.
When the conversation at the table turned liquid,

I moved back to the corner to study the tar
an artist laid thick with her hands

and each grain stalk lodged in the rough coat of marrow,
but aligned like consternations of light.

I still cannot stop seeing
the trembling lines, or the cracked pitch

clutching each plait of grain.
Or the way Alice kept darkening.

How each night before she enters to sleep,
she must study the wall of her primitive self.

After a tart with plucked berries patterned on top,
she helped us on with our coats. It was winter,

a reduced palette of light, a sequence,
an immutable anatomy of long narrow marks.

Homeostasis: Night

When I can't sleep
I ask you to tell me a story
though I am all grown up

and I listen
to what it was like
to be a boy
that one year
in southern Illinois,
how you loved snow
and your bike
and where your house was
at the end of a lane
and how you found that house
because of a man
at a gas station

but then I fall asleep
and don't know
what happens next.

Gin

The day's first gin is throat dry. Sharp
    and pure. Ice

        still whole when
he gets another. He drinks

        until the angle of half-
light is lost. Until the glass
      is asleep by

  the door and the glass
     empty and the glass
       carried. The mind

       floats and widens
    beyond anything bio-

logical. The mind
    with its musical
       light never surfacing. The
    never mind. Infused

  in an abyss deeper
     than the mind
  until his body

is only this
  and fleeing the body with-
     in his body
  and the damage is also parched
    like this.

Fiction

Every Wednesday
he is mourner and bitter

in time beneath pardon.
Long glasses fill

to the neck
until the table is liquid.

His voice is a hand
cupping the ocean.

He is shirking his love.

He is loving his love. He says *love*
to a wife but it isn't

love that has fallen
into the glass.

It's a mouth wearing a fiction,

a mouth already dry.
He sighs and says

he'll be home on his white legs
but lands instead

where he's willing to feather
and wing each passage,

where he swallows
each way of pretending.

Black Place

INSPIRED BY GEORGIA O'KEEFFE, *BLACK PLACE, GREY AND PINK*, 1949, OIL ON CANVAS

I sit between black lava and ash

dust-brushed and shaken
amid suggestion of bone

in the curve of the place without sky

rose-lipped clouds

first grinding of pigment and palette

      knife
      broken pastel
      a thousand forms of time

Quench

What I never needed
folded out before me
on a table by the bar Sometimes
we never stopped
sitting We sat
detached or rapt in the hush
under the low yellow
vocation of light and pronounced
swallows with a rigor of sinking We wasted
whatever we could of the day
and the prized light made me
more peachy I was promise To him
I was ear and action
he could have where we sat
but right now he was clasped
in the maze of drops
on his tongue and waiting
for seize to release He needed this
more than me and wiped his lips
with what he preferred He needed
each trace taken up The man bent his body
toward the glass and he chewed
on the liquid and counted
as the liquid crowded inside
until it became the map
of his simple his heaven

The Bed on the Wall

INSPIRED BY ROBERT RAUSCHENBERG, *BED*, 1955,
OIL AND PENCIL MARKINGS ON PILLOW, QUILT AND SHEET

So garish: the arc of his interior
thinking. So red,

so deceptive. The coordinates of this project fall
between sheets and box spring:

the command of horizontal passage.
The bed soaked

with the overlapping tongue
of his brushes, with pattern interruption, the departure

from edges. Let's say he is within
his composition. Inside

his story. As he tips
the paint, the objective can be taken

altogether away until he detects
only desire: a rough strike

of purple
censured from exuberance. The room remains

with the weeping wreckage
all around, and the panels

in the corner
beaded with aggressive desperate skins.

Below the window, the dirty
city, its permanent

tensed distances, its hungry
catastrophes, its bare

windows. His pillow is creased. It tells everything
we need to know. Each drip, directionless.

A Normal Week

I believe I've earned what isn't yet
bitter. This whole town hides ghosts,
and my first sip is the last measure.
I find the setting conducive,
such an elegant empire

of forks. Even the knives hold
their judgments. No more than slicing.
We are accommodating the room,
and the room is not rushing.
The cup is empty. How desperate

weakening can be. We both have
houses with windows where we lie
in every tossed night. We might be
recuperating from darkness—the bend
at the stairs, the crack in each hour.

Here, we receive the fruit brought
to the table. We accept organ meats
and small plates of cream.
I lick the whole day and my belly fills.
The candles crackle back. I remember
nothing and nothing comes after me.

~

So what if you get wet, he says, soaked in desperation.

Swainson's Hawk

White throat and pointed wings, a perch
in Spanish bayonet, in shinnery oak, in pasture.

Small eyes tucking in to prey. I always forget
the haste of dismantling

the torn-off evidence:
leopard lizard, whiptail, kestrel, shrike.

While stars are raw, a raptor feathered to the toes
will eat grasped rats and voles,

collect the flapping bats. Another bone,
another funeral. The supply nearly endless.

I'm arriving on time to a table.
The mouth holds sorrows. Teeth cling to the soundless:

the leaves and route, the sunset rushes by.
Somewhere, a rabbit warm in the hawk's beak.

A Glass

We never
discuss

but
right there
while I am hankering

for a glass

he is drinking five
with his insignificant mouth

We are moving toward linger

longer reminded
of an instant
uttered again

Let the other

woman be identical let her be exhausted
in pretty in soiling let her not be too
lonely let her protect what she knows and let
one take blood from the other let one see each
later version let her never keep her eyes
open let them both have a chance to be tender
in the beautiful rooms let them be strangers
with distance let each rearrange the heart
let there be viscera and once and fact
and fierce pattern let the hints happen little
by little let the one scream let there be sleeves
of rain let her open a map and decide to move
forward let each form from the heavy edges
in the black part of night

Instead—Small, Rather Huddled and So On

INSPIRED BY EVA HESSE'S ARTWORKS, INCLUDING *REPETITION NINETEEN III*, 1968, FIBERGLASS AND RESIN

Why this pile of parts, the resin-soaked heads
tightening? From her hands

on air, the suggestion of body. I wander
in this room of spines, but leave

them alone. Such guts: the presence of versus
and peril. Against self-sacrifice she gestured,

contoured. Against the silver in her head.
The rope, the line, absurd: a penis, then pink

relief. I move around to find what's left:
smoothings and soft orbs. Nineteen repetitions, wan,

translucent. Lapped with wax
or liquid latex, cheesecloth, rubber. From her hands,

the gathered moods. Her resin,
tube-like, glowing. And now, the sun pierces

a small window because sometimes
we need defenses. I let it parse and wait

a little longer. All the surfaces keep
kneeling, standing. Holy, hollow,

dossing down. When I close my eyes,
the pieces reconnoiter, occupy the grieving

room. Her forms are shaded
in their seam and volume. Each time,

she climbed to what was meaningless
and gave it flexion. Is it refusal to accuse

the eye of what it's doing, adding
life to puckers, to the flaying folds?

Each time, she must have laughed,
then dripped discharge and aberration.

Answers to Why

In the forest we idled
the car as a multiplied moon slipped
from the envelope of sky. I couldn't say *no*—
no wasn't an option he offered
so the word lived in silence
with its lost potential. My low voice
not yet folded in its shadow
of ruin and I swallowed, phrasing
the pearl and sequence
of surrender. When later he ordered
a long line of wines, sweet
with murmur and grasping, I tried
to remain neutral with irrefutable
shrugs. How little I knew.
Listen, I was dissolving. An ongoing
volatility enveloped the inside
of my thighs. I didn't know to limit
the damage, so sipped again
in the careless slow light.
The table wished to be between us.
We held it. We took comfort
in not understanding our saturated
hearts. Outside,
the sun covered itself.
From the beginning we did not discipline
our words. Each was each
of the reasons: October, November,
winter, wincing. Outside, birds kept arriving
hour on hour. The blunt blue sky.
Gazes had grazed my body before.
I thought I could handle this.
To myself, I kept only
the most precious trembling.

Golden Eagle

Nearly silent from the cliff,
the great bird unties his wings in curves and rolls

through open air. Such searching.
He lowers to find flesh, his silhouette obedient

to the sky's bewildered blue.
Patrol, tilt. In 3-2-1

the route turns perpendicular.
His narrow awful face

quickens on perishable landscape,
everything in the open—

pitches and voices. Some echoes.
He grabs enough for one. Ignores the moan.

At the table, was I greedy?
I hardly ate. Only what I needed.

Flavor

I'd been careful all my life.
That day I wore my carmine shirt. Suddenly his jaw,

the table, the large room.
Many hands waiting to offer comfort.

Where the walls sang, hours were fine
and the wine lazy, the taste

of punishment
as strong and sweet as pardon.

Days at Zero

Pursuit

Let me take you to bed with the end of my head...

Consider his elbow as he leans into my syntax.

If, several years later, I pursue
the reason I drifted
from where I live, only saucers and wine glasses

will know of the dialogue, the pulsing—
Flesh again.
Not that I remember.

So many photographs
of blank images. I was always sodden
in the slow empire of time.

Not to Not

In an alley, we swerve unhurried into stars, kiss the calcium-rich light
of the crescent moon. He hands me his madness and I arch, all sinew

and lava, all watermelon sugar. I murmur marred words

to his threadbare shadow in tiny constellations until each sentence
is the wet claim of want packed into bricks and pots,

a fragrant bloom of desire. I must not be distracted by the bottle and his cup
of kisses, the blue sardonic laugh of his flesh and this uncertain commerce

of lust, the infinite haste for his hands on my body.

I cannot gather such flourishes, the casual spill into intricacy with its bulbous
afternoons of sighing. If he asks to pray at the altar of anticipation

where craving becomes motion, widening again into wine until the waitress
has come to our table seven times and the glass remains empty, gleaming,

the law of distraction must not settle in. A thousand times,

I'll refuse to return, but we are each part animal, each invisible,
poured into impurity by thirst, an invasion of the margin.

Impatient as I am to get away, if the glass holds my hand,
I will bring my voice to the place he draws his need,

and he'll become my talon and my shadow, someone I'll oblige.

So What If You Over and Over

I knew
I'd come
back
that day I was
downtown when
I should have
been home
which was all
couldn'ts
and *shoulds*
and has occupied me
ever since

I entered the bar
without
words I entered
the roux
of a dark
where fat questions
of virtue
were slung
on the back
of a chair—
the edges
of skin the barren

landscape
and in there
a palace Everything
in me and our large
sips It was
never far
to the place
between tolerance
and guilt—and
I hardly tried
to climb out
of my ways.

Drops

His fingers collect my sweet sap
and I paint the bed

with a dozen drops
of blood. One window without

chambers. The phone rings twice
as the wine glass watches

from the table, and
calls out with questions.

Begin again
with sorrow. For this is

how we feed
ourselves, wrapped

in the silken
accumulation of lies,

how we bend
through invisible reason.

What is formed can vanish
in rustle, but the room

is full of flavors,
and even under-

nourished, I hide
the face of loss, knowing

that he'll rinse
his mouth and the protein-

rich secretion
of remorse, which keeps seeping,

knowing
that he watches it

sluice the shiny surface
of the porcelain.

A Brief History of Coyotes

Set the dark to hushing.
Beyond our house, their muzzles.

In the year of long pollen
where aggression sinks its crusts and clouds turn

to flesh-horizon, we come undone indoors.
Canines thread through mortared light

imposing their congested howls.
We hear their blades and hollows from the bottom

of the night. Wings unfurl from branches.
Feathers find their angles.

Next, the claws and gullies, the valley feeding.
Wind moves without good reason.

Listening through the wall,
we've knuckled back to silence.

Insomnia

Middle of each night,
the man reads pages of hours
and chapters while a gray moon slips
to a triangle of pebbles.

He hefts his wide novel
from the previous repeat, leaves the ruffle
of stretched sheets and slips to the couch,
erasing the deep sense of sleep.
His eyes feel absurd,
flensed of matter in heavy-
lidded surrender. On it goes—

discard all minutes.
Watch shapes shade the wall
and a yellow haze from the overheads.

Exhaustion relaxes
in messy piles, and the cat
melts to her malaise, back of the sofa
with that dark, drooping curtain of fur.

Hours are dying
in the half-carcassed night.
Through a fog of exhaustion,
the man takes a protean range
of elixirs and tinctures,
and what is held finally eases, erases:

the thick sky and its edge,
the maddening chartreuse of the clock.
He snores, boiled or frozen by night,
puts his back to the pink bloom
of quick-starting sun.

He'll get a few hours
before day skims the window.
Before other bolts and holdings

let loose. Before the light is proportional,
expanding. Before the horizon
flips up from the dark.

Hush Again

Wild strawberry had been rising from rocky places.
On the street small boys in red.
Above them on poles some crows.

A delphinium,
a bartender,
a hundred times.

Failed to joy, I fell
a year. No one saw my blurs and constellations.

A swirl of streets slurred to summer rain.
How many slants of light
in the intimate alphabet? I knew them all.

Looking back—
two chairs and thirsty people, small leftover goals.

My tongue still willing to tongue whatever words.

Three

The sky landed
on the mountains while I
lapped at the vessel Every day
seemed full of thereafter I wanted
the room tilting Those afternoons were all
appetite My chair next to his
chair where we could shunt life's
punctures aside The first one
wanted me home He wanted to be
calmer He wanted me not to collect
other people Why not be honest Why
not say we were all secretly suffocating
in whispers and we each needed
beyond So we took whatever was worst
and that hour and the next and unlucky
the next And stayed
all of us exhausted We were
lonely and boundless in this
exploring The sun meant
to say something about
the spread of horizon but
we couldn't hear it couldn't
stop fleshing in barter
or feeling the cold
crawling in

Sharp-shinned Hawk

Days are barely at zero.
Take wind shear as the palace, pleasure layer, depth.

The bird raises its head from a chest soft with down.
From above, the land is scars

sewn with narrow eyes. Steady, steady—
it swerves and lurks

in hackberry, soapberry, mesquite.
As if one could ride a sun to luck.

One does. Behold.
Between flaps and gliding, it nests inside

some tighter aspen branches. Eats first
crickets as small delicacy before its centered eyes

triangulate on songbirds: sparrow, thrush
in gentle grass. Bounty, bounty, bounty.

Juice and Distillation

We sat shoulder to shoulder over the sugared
cuisine, and the raw and the salted.

I love you, I do, he said, and I sighed.

If I was nectar, he was parched,
a body without doubt, and later, tasting

with the sharp knife what had been unseeded.
The harvest was plentiful that year.

Whether

Tell me why being there was always ending.
       Tell it four times or six.

I'm back to the twang of a body and its declaration.

I'm not revealing the gaps, the familiar
       repeating strange without echoes,

but want to remember driving into the mountains
       when there was hardly snow.

Fluid

We drove twice to the mountains and endless
times east as sun riffled cross-eyed past juniper.

We drove ourselves slow in our desert
and the ground around us rolled

out of being. Forget about thinking;
we were spoonfuls

of liquid. We left one container
and entered another: a glass to a glass.

We couldn't get further. We tracked
our demands across tables, fortified

by enzymes and acids and sediment.
We were moving the bottom, increasing the ratio:

wine to time. We spoke verbs
without words. The man aged

in the bottle. He existed
so I poured and leaned in and maintained.

Once was Lost

And this is how it is
And how this is

It is and this is his And I was born
with this and how is it this

Is how it is

I Recommend You Not Empty of Content

When I stood and tore rocks
from the edge of our porch, you saw I was otherwise
empty of details, of spark. From words to cup
to hope to wake: you called for help.

From the edge of our porch, you saw I was otherwise
caught in the arch of defeat. No chances
to hope to wake. You called for help
that day. October was visible in every direction,

caught in the arch of defeat. No chances.
How many times could we do this? I almost slid off
that day. October was visible in every direction,
taut then shaking. Was this on your heart?

How many times could we do this? I almost slid off
from the place we called home. Pity the riddle,
taut then shaking. Was this on your heart —
your sturdy going on, your exhaustion

with the place we called home? Pity the riddle,
empty of details, of spark. From words to cup,
your sturdy going on, your exhaustion
when I stood and tore rocks.

Empirical Theories of a Box-Maker

INSPIRED BY DONALD JUDD'S 100 UNTITLED WORKS HOUSED AT THE CHINATI FOUNDATION,
MARFA, TEXAS, 1982-86, MILL ALUMINUM

☐

In the prairie grass, a revision of rigor in sunrise and terminating hours. On concrete floor, desolation. These are the breath of the box, the plural of what's been placed. A hundred the same repetitions how many times that make it possible to understand that the sky wanders.

☐

A century of boxes looking for daylight or moonborder. In each box, I separate distance. Look through. See what's been emptied.

☐

After a day at the boxes you want what isn't. Next, and next. Next, and next. You think you are walking, but instead you are waking backwards, linking revelations together and waiting for the room to stop disclosing its fissures.

☐ ☐ ☐ ☐

The boxes have been abandoned   or are full

☐

—says Malevich
the white free abyss, infinity, is before you

In the boxes any view
is what you will tolerate

after three windstorms the boxes
hold the geography of what sways us

□

this untitled box of choices this untitled box of daylight this untitled box of exoneration this untitled box of absence this untitled box of perfection this untitled box of averting your eyes this untitled box of grudges this untitled box of caution this untitled box of trees this untitled box of confessing this untitled box of resemblance this untitled box of volume this untitled box of duty this untitled box of what's already formed this untitled box of denial this untitled box of days to never remember this untitled box of isolation this untitled box of dust or of dusk this untitled box of voices this untitled box of translucence this untitled box of hours this untitled box of suggestion this untitled box of glances this untitled box of intolerable heat this untitled box of rules this untitled box of corner office this untitled box of prairie this untitled box of infinite cues this untitled box of not even one glass this untitled box of slow motion this untitled box of tangle this untitled box of reflection this untitled box of exits this untitled box of parallel sides this untitled box of permission this untitled box of accidents this untitled box of signals this untitled box with dark heavy corners this untitled box of flaws this untitled box of air this untitled box of precision this untitled box of yellow lines on the road this untitled box of authority this untitled box of sediment this untitled box of margins this untitled box of variation this untitled box of contact this untitled box of succumbing this untitled box of responses this untitled box of insistence this untitled box of vision this untitled box of why you sat there week after week this untitled box of paying the bill this untitled box of despites this untitled box of intersection this untitled box of small favors this untitled box of clouds landing multiple this untitled box of borders this untitled box of wallet and napkin this untitled box of alleys this untitled box of returning this untitled box of sorrow this untitled box of the night this untitled box of the tense tear of conscience this untitled box of sentences we said at the table this untitled box of the next thing you order this untitled box of what's been taken this untitled box of canyons this untitled box of touching this untitled box of yesterday this untitled box of ravens on poles this untitled box of together this untitled box of supposing this untitled box of white china plates this untitled box of shadow this untitled box of yes and again yes this untitled box of constraint this untitled box of what you are capable of this untitled box of low wind this untitled box of murmurs this untitled box of the rest of it this untitled box of how many this untitled box of fluttering senses this untitled box of simplicity this untitled box of a wedding ring in a small box this untitled box of this morning this untitled box of forgetting this untitled box of potential this untitled box of silence this untitled box of what we long for and what we get this untitled box of order this untitled box of questions this untitled box of truth and how that doesn't help this untitled box of clamor this untitled box of sight this untitled box of the body this untitled box of thereafter and windows that lead out to nothing this untitled box of where the hand ends this untitled box of containing this untitled box of conversion of hovering next to yourself of looking beyond or into of absence of enter

These are the intricate
whole holes unguarded
to which you are admitted

You see I have opened other domains to you

In these boxes, we are back at the argument of existence, a substance of space, all of it constructed. I've said what is possible in tall grass reflections.

Sun strikes this box as an object of trespass.

☐

Out of a point, a lack, an opposite vertical
for your intimacies and judgments.

☐

—a box empty of anything but box. What
I can't measure—first light final
light how the earth rotates. If someone asked you for some part
of yourself and you never before realized
the flat light of knowing, you could learn
to enclose words without words, to box up the intervals.

☐ ☐ ☐ ☐

the dark is never at the top

☐

traces of mirror repeat the storm-
flecked Trans-Pecos West Texas

now it is raining each box filled with field filled
with sagebrush all of it in the boxes

in particular detail in the boxes
the steel desert-blushing and haunted

you hear it the closer
you get to the boxes the light tidying life
and otherwise keep looking

at long recall all there ever was
is linear on that side or that opening

☐

When we build, we put walls on the innermost. On your way out of the desert, stop by
the edge of the road—and look at the rusted hide of husked fields against one another.
All places are good, all places savage. I thought Celan said it best that our roots are stuck
in the air where they remain. Look at the flowers specifically the daisies that grow loose
as sand twists and spirals. Look at the clouds seared white with nothing gripping the sky.

Perennials

Each time I left the dark room, I took
the bones of roses
                    that had once grown
        in the alley. I took

the tinted water and the succulent sun. So strong

was my need that I then took the pale moon. Filled
eight pockets with pressures. Already I was tired, but I took

and continued. Less exact
and more needy. Because I was opened

by another, I will always carry these remnants of pouring light

in my body. I must remember that my mind was disrobing
            and this wasn't pleasure, but loss

growing like a bud. I returned

past culverts and tree limbs, past the flesh
of dry fields, I returned, wanting to live

in the future,
                to praise its perfection. I returned empty, without.

Common Raven

Even on the main road, black wing
and gloss. A call without such sorrow.

Wheel ruts in nameless light. Snow cold.
How long until you land,

each feather fluffed with the faithless world?
There is such ungodliness

in what the tongue will feed on.
You make the road a table,

demand pleasure in ransom,
bragging your laws with glottal stops.

And now, the gorge—
the eye, skin, leg. As tires move by,

your endless chewing.
It seems like rage, but it is only hunger.

Defenses

We're in double reverse and trying
      to be better sensible.
            All the workers drag past our table:
      janitors, dishwashers, barkeep.
Curl, swivel, anchor.

Through the small windows,
      the desert keeps pouring from mountains.
            Wind chimes get louder, the heart darker.
      After he arrives, I can't wait to stay.
Hours spill over. A clock without hesitation.

Qualms

With wine, I went right
to the open mouth,

took it down, familiar
with the charm of my own particular

sin. It was as if
I had already all the history

of my two worlds,
morning and later—

another street I wouldn't
have to recognize. Or maybe

those were only
suspicions of conscience.

Little difference the lexicon
if the sense were the mouth of another.

Each half of the day
drunk twice, and no thought

about pauses. Each luxury
of sublingual darkness.

Long sentences
smoothed by spoons.

We sat in our eyes.
One of two was chorus, one held out

his glass at the same time,
emptying nothing. I went home

with peaches after,
with a mind of delay.

Best Portrait

INSPIRED BY THE PHOTOGRAPHY OF ANNIE LIEBOVITZ

In the morning
with her largest lens, each frame
allows a sudden opening. She climbs the ladder—
eyes, shoulders, skin.
It is a long walk to the end of a face.

In the afternoon,
image becomes excursion, the pleasure
of finding the shape of a stranger in the curve
of a lens. Nothing shelters the shot.
No distraction.

Each gesture is bundled
in whispers. The evening's penitent
light, and the hard eye
of flash leads to rumor.
Then the picture spills out by itself.

The Narrator is Always Nameless

I gave my fur and all my contours

and off he went, inside my thighs,
to make the smallest circles

with impatience, seeking flowers,
blooms. A nod began the name of all my senses.

The gesture bending in. *Bring another*, he said,

and many more.

Again the world could take a moment.

Inward, Downward: White, Gray, Black

INSPIRED BY PIET MONDRIAN, *COMPOSITION NO. II*, 1920, OIL ON CANVAS

the box in the middle opens a door to
the pond
                                in his
                            backyard
where no one ever quarrels

the sun elbows the red fence with loose
gate-post in the back alley
                        and tender cold air

from the side yard
            comes to meet   the sweet
                        and endless blooms

Heaping Dusk

At the edge of our fiction there were rows of delphinium Every week I wanted most to be limitless and he wanted another turn of the glass combined with my best diction I could have predicted what mouths soothe and how many chances what I almost abandoned the bramble the prisms of ruin but saw another great day with rows of delphinium and yes I clogged up with endearment and loosed my fleet alphabet at the table Later in the glow around night I dreamt of violent bird wings of hunting and hiding of meat scraps but by day the glass again swam to the skin and the precise grasses outside were without feature to my anyone clutching my body in the heaping dusk I came back again retracing my swallows with proof that I was still amused Never mind how the door opened inward It was the voice of the wine the red incentive that I found imperative To be honest I had never owned elegance and needed each trivial hand of it The street grew its blue delphinium and dusk reappeared in the darkness Before long I remained with the ache and the spark and he was the glass But isn't it silly to tell you we held its confusions and for a while I thought each of those days was filled with repose I was fragile as we fed on the inevitable question as our landscape restructured became hesitation The crevice of my heart I left hidden and probably this story is filled with exact gaps and familiar motivations and anyway the delphinium kept spinning my moods

Ask Yourself

Out there the moon is lunatic.
Beneath floorboards, rats build piles of mosses.

The cat drags birds to the porch, often cataloguing carcasses.

Many times awe, then stupid variables.

Every dawn, I remade the bed with urgency.
Then returned through the cobalt canvas sky.

Excavation

We consumed with both hands, tasting the pig
or sweet onion. Coaxed
the raw to our mouths. What had barely begun,

the long line of plates. We asked for the sugared
then *No, not enough.* We asked again
in the emptiness. He said *If you drive off forever, the world,*

which was perfect will become various.
A motorcycle passed
in the hollows of our breathing. Every night

all the language a terrain not as terrible
as the thrashing of meat from our spit.
Please, can we have some more fatty questions,

a table to the left? How obvious we were.
More of the musk
of such clutching, and where to put his signature

in me. As if we had already lost everything,
we requested every cream,
every greed. My whole body was warm

in the mouth, starved for its grief.
I would have eaten whatever was most bloody,
and held my hand to my throat.

Equivalent

Witch's broom, a half-broken memory.
Formation of ravens as evidence. This is the respite

from hesitance, and the chance to watch sky
thirsting for heartbroken clouds.
The ground remains nearly expressionless.

The sun has been churning.
I type nine goodbyes in a white room.

Tomorrow I'll have something in common
with those who once lived here:
the warm sound of old wounds.

The knife upside-down in the kitchen, the jawbone
on a fence on the hillside, and the man
with a shaker of salt. It will all stay the same.

Wild horses, a hedge of cobwebs.
Now, the man with a needle, pulling out droplets of blood.
The sun lands as ash in the bath.

Great Horned Owl

It is almost time. Where the owl sits, a scrawled moon
glorifies his back. The horizon has become trees

in a line, the lines inside a din of winter.
He assumes the yellow-eyed stare

of the ravenous. His stuttering call drops
from snags and ledges. Now, the owl's cloak of gray

vaults the road. We can hardly breathe. Such bracing.
We know what it is to pursue prey, to be pursued,

to offer others our softest feathers.
The bird rides the clean dry cold

to another movement, another seize in the ghostly night.
At the dinner table, we listen

to the ripping. The grip is fierce. Finished,
the owl rests—sovereign, and we do not want to see.

Homeostasis: Birdwatching

The kisses you left on my shoulder are soft
bird tears. Today when you spread
my legs open, claiming me, folding
yourself into the hidden droplets
of my body, the broken birds flew out
with a monstrous cry. We were wrinkled
with sweat and breath and found
love again at our palms. My body praised
and tensed as bodies do and yours
staggered and learned again to sigh
and turn and then we looked outside
at green on green three acres
of bindweed rose petals new mornings.

Homeostasis: Autumn

A day that stayed in place, inaudible from dawn to the strike of evening.
Enough time to rest and plunge back across the pebbles
        to my pens and desk.
A squash we didn't plant has come in gold across the aspen roots.
Two hawks burst over, claiming a rotating sky.
The desert, normally dry, emits a faint scent, the damp wisp of cedar.
Water has gathered in holes we dug.
This is why the pangs of time are necessary.
To the east, mountains bracket the distance, releasing their images
        silver on blue.
The whole day has nearly disappeared and night is a ruffle about to blossom.

Acknowledgments

The author wishes to acknowledge the editors of the following publications in which these poems first appeared, some in different forms or with different titles:

About Place Journal — "Great Horned Owl"
Adobe Walls Anthology — "A Glass"
American Chordata — "I Recommend You Not Empty of Content"
Avatar Review — "Insomnia"
Belmont Story Review — "Swainson's Hawk"
Beloit Poetry Journal — "Whether"
Central Avenue — "Homeostasis: Night"
Clade Song — "A Brief History of Coyotes"
Connotation Press: An Online Artifact — "Answers to Why"
Cutthroat — "Common Raven"
Edwin E. Smith's Quarterly Magazine — "Appetite" and "So What If You Over and Over"
Ekphrasis — "Tar Painting"
Eleven Eleven — "Perennials"
Interim — "Excavation"
Leveler — "Heaping Dusk"
Memorious — "Instead—Small, Rather Huddled and So On"
Muzzle— "Gin"
New American Writing — "Pursuit"
New Mexico Mercury — "Black Place"
Not Drowning, Waving — "Homeostasis: Birdwatching"
One — "A Normal Week"
Parcel — "Three"
Perfume River Poetry Review — "Not to Not"
Poem-a-Day (Academy of American Poets) — "The Bed on the Wall"
Prime Number — "The Night Clouds Wrestled the Sky" and "Fiction"
Puerto del Sol — "Drops"
Redactions — "Hush, Then"
Redheaded Stepchild — "Fluid"
Rogue Agent — "Smote"
Salamander — "Juice and Distillation"
Santa Fe Literary Review — "Draw a Box"
Taos Journal of International Poetry & Art — "Let the other"
The Collapsar — "Qualms"
The Ilanot Review — "Quench"

The Journal — "Hush Again"
The Perch — "Find the Color of Survival"
The Seattle Review — "Empirical Theories of a Box-Maker"
Trailer Park Quarterly — "Splendid"
Two Peach — "Repetitions"
Weber — "Homeostasis: Autumn"

"Leather World, This Bird, This Sky" and "Equivalent" were among a selection of five poems that won the RaedLeaf Poetry-India 2014 Award (International).

"Leather World, This Bird, This Sky" was reprinted in *OCELLI*.

The epigraph is drawn from an interview of Eva Hesse by Cindy Nemser that first appeared in *Artforum* 8, no. 9 (May 1970).

Thank you to Tupelo Press for believing in this book and making it real.

Finally, with tenderness for David and our lucky days together.

Lauren Camp is the author of five books of poems. She received the Dorset Prize and finalist citations for the Arab American Book Award and the New Mexico-Arizona Book Award. She came to poetry while working as a visual artist, a career she has since left behind. Camp lives in New Mexico, where she teaches creative writing to people of all ages. *www.laurencamp.com*

Recent and Selected Titles from Tupelo Press

Native Voices: Indigenous American Poetry, Craft and Conversations (anthology), edited by CMarie Fuhrman & Dean Rader

What Could Be Saved: Bookmatched Novellas and Stories (fiction), Gregory Spatz

Kill Class (poems), Nomi Stone

Dancing in Odessa (poems), Ilya Kaminsky

Hazel (novel), David Huddle

Epistle, Osprey (poems), Geri Doran

Franciscan Notes (poetry/memoir), Alan Williamson

A Certain Roughness in Their Syntax (poems), Jorge Aulicino, translated by Judith Filc

Flight (poems), Chaun Ballard

Another English: Anglophone Poems from Around the World (anthology), edited by Catherine Barnett and Tiphanie Yanique

The Book of LIFE (poems), Joseph Campana

Fire Season (poems), Patrick Coleman

New Cathay: Contemporary Chinese Poetry (anthology), edited by Ming Di

Calazaza's Delicious Dereliction (poems), Suzanne Dracius, translated by Nancy Naomi Carlson

Gossip and Metaphysics: Russian Modernist Poetry and Prose (anthology), edited by Katie Farris, Ilya Kaminsky, and Valzhyna Mort

See our complete list at www.tupelopress.org